To Brian

# IN THE MOMENT

To all the many memorable moments shared & to be shared.

Love & blessings

Robert.

# IN THE MOMENT

inspiration for a new millennium

**Robert Silverstone**

**Unlimited Publishing**
Bloomington, Indiana

Copyright © 2001 by Robert Silverstone

Distributing Publisher:
Unlimited Publishing, LLC
Bloomington, Indiana
http://www.unlimitedpublishing.com

Book and Cover Design by Charles King
Copyright © 2001 by Unlimited Publishing, LLC
This book was typeset with Adobe® InDesign™, using the Adobe Garamond® typeface.

Cover image "Sunrise Moment" and interior photos by Robert Silverstone
Copyright © 2001 by Robert Silverstone

All rights reserved under Title 17, U.S. Code, International and Pan-American Copyright Conventions. No part of this work may be reproduced or transmitted in any form or by any means, electronic or mechanical, including photocopying, scanning, recording or duplication by any information storage or retrieval system without prior written permission from the author(s) and publisher(s), except for the inclusion of brief quotations with attribution in a review or report. Requests for permission or further information should be addressed to the author(s).

Unlimited Publishing LLC provides worldwide book design, printing, marketing and distribution services for professional writers and small to mid-size presses, serving as distributing publisher. Sole responsibility for the content of each work rests with the author(s) and/or contributing publisher(s). The opinions expressed herein may not be interpreted in any way as representing those of Unlimited Publishing, nor any of its affiliates.

ISBN 1-58832-014-6

*For more information
about the author or the
photographs seen in this book
please contact the publisher
or visit
www.inthemoment.net*

*Dedicated to bringing alive*

*the spirit of the moment*

*that dwells within each one of us*

*"Each moment
is a brush stroke
on the canvas
that becomes
the masterpiece
of our lives."*

—Robert Silverstone

# IN THE MOMENT

# TABLE OF CONTENTS

ACKNOWLEDGMENTS • xi
INTRODUCTION • 3

## PART I — IN THE MOMENT OF LIFE

MOMENT BY MOMENT • 9
NOW • 10
THIS IS THE TIME • 12
THE DRAMA • 13
THE BOX • 14
STEP OUT OF THE MIST • 15
THE SPIRIT OF THE NIGHT • 16
NOW IS ALWAYS HERE • 17
THE SPIRAL TURNS • 18
FROM TIME TO TIME • 19
THE SOUL OF THE NIGHT • 20
ANOTHER YEAR GONE BY • 21
IT … • 22
THE STORM BELOW • 23
PLEASE DON'T TRY • 24
ONE STEP BACK • 25
WANDERING • 26
IT'S TIME • 28
THEY SAID … • 30
NEW YEAR • 32
MONSTERS IN THE DARK • 33
LIKE IT … OR NOT • 34
FOOTPRINTS ON THE WATER • 35
MOONSTAR • 36
A DRAMA • 38
THE CITY • 41

TURBULENCE • 42
IF EVER … • 44

## PART II — IN THE MOMENT OF SELF

MOMENT OF THANKS • 49
PICTURE PUZZLE • 50
I AM HERE • 52
PASSAGE OF TIME • 53
WALK ALONE • 54
HEY WORLD • 55
DEMONS OF THE MORNING • 56
RAGING STORM • 58
SIGNS • 59
THE CALM • 60
THANKS • 61
COLORS • 62
ANGELS OF THE SKY • 64
THE POWER WITHIN • 65
WINDOW SEAT • 66
MASTER OF THE MOMENT • 68

## PART III — IN THE MOMENT OF TRUTH

TRUTHS ABOUT LIFE • 73
MY GUIDES • 74
CLOSE YOUR EYES • 75
THE LAST TIME • 76
DREAMS COME TRUE • 77
A CLEANSING • 78
THE CHALLENGE • 80
OPEN YOUR EYES • 82
THE GIFT • 84
LET IT GO • 87
YESTERDAY • 88

YOU CAN FEEL IT · 90
YOU KNOW HOW · 92
LOVE YOUR SELF · 93

## IN THE MOMENT
· 95

## SLICE IT AWAY
· 103

## WE ARE YOU
· 117

## DON'T STOP … KEEP GOING
· 125

# ACKNOWLEDGMENTS

This book has been in the "making" for many years. When I stop to think of just how many years, I must really go back to my childhood in England. To my parents, who dreamed of me becoming a doctor or a lawyer, a "professional man," for that would have made them proud, and would have provided me with the "security" they never knew. I must first thank them. Had it not been for the loss of my parents in my early years, I may never have commenced this journey. That experience, though traumatic and painful at times, eventually opened my mind to the realization that "everything happens for a reason" and that "there are no bad reasons." Thank you Mum and Dad, I love you both and I hope this makes you proud.

My thanks, love and prayers go out to my beautiful sister, Michele, for being my parent when they were not there, for being my spiritual mirror, for loving me and helping me to discover my own inner strength. To my dear brother-in-law, Michael, who gave me my "Donald Duck," which has served me well over the years. To my darling nieces, Debby and Vikki, who have taught me so much as I observe them exploring their own adventures.

Limitless and eternal gratitude to my Nena, whose demonstration of unconditional love and support for me and this work helped put the final pieces into place.

It is with deep appreciation that I honor and respect Kelly, who created the sacred and safe environment for this work to flourish, and whose loving "nudges" helped bring it to fruition.

Thanks to Dennis, Phil, Barry, Ruth and a most special thanks to Stephen, Carrie and Jovial, whose unfailing belief in me and unlimited support encouraged me to complete the work which began all those years ago.

To Nikos, my dear friend, who reassured me that spirit can survive in the business world. To Deborah Cooper, who helped dispel my clouds of uncertainty during my transitional time. To Rusty Berkus, whose own inspirational words gave positive support to this work. Thanks to my friend Chris, who helped teach me to "breathe." To all my business colleagues, associates and clients whose support has provided me with the freedom to release my creative spirit. It has been through the lessons they have presented, that I have learned to detach from the "drama" and stay "in the moment" of it all.

To all my many dear friends and family members who have touched my life in so many extraordinary ways. All have helped contribute to the self realization of who I really am. It is my wish and prayer for them all that they discover the place of peace, calm and happiness that I have discovered, and am continuing to experience every day of my journey.

To Julia Cameron, Mark Bryan, Neale Donald Walsch, Maryann Williamson, Dr. Carolyn Myss, Dr. Deepak Choprah, Kahil Gibran, Paramahansa Yogananda, Alan Cohen, Dr. Scott Peck, Dr. Wayne Dyer, Arnold Patent, Jack Canfield, Thomas Moore, Barbara Marx Hubbard and other respected teachers. Their writings, spirit, truth and beliefs have been a source of inspiration, opening doors and illuminating the way, while walking this tightrope of my spiritual path.

My gratitude to those special individuals who have been a pillar of strength to me as I explored the boundaries of my soul. Those named and unnamed, known and unknown, seen and unseen angels and guides who have always been there when I've needed them the most. They have touched my heart, lifted my spirit, helped restore my faith, and kept me on the right path, as I ventured out and pursued this journey.

Finally, my thanks to my God, my Great Creator, my Inner Guide, my Mentor, who has provided for all these gifts and abundance of the universe to come to me and flow through me. You have been my light when there was darkness, my inspiration when there was doubt, my intuition when I was undecided, my faith when there was fear, my love when I was in pain. Thank you for answering my prayers and for making my dreams come true. You have proved to me that faith and love are really all we need, and that all we ever need, we already have. I am truly in your eternal grace.

# IN THE MOMENT

# INTRODUCTION

*In the Moment* is a journey within. It is a fantastic voyage, full of dreams and visions, truths and ideas, that resonate deep in our souls. In order to embark on this journey we must first liberate ourselves from certain conditioning that Western culture has permeated into our consciousness. Whether through the mediums of newspapers or television, movies or magazines, we have all grown up in a society which has cultivated attachments to the physical and material aspects of everyday life ... to things that change.

The more we have unconsciously become attached to these trappings, the further we have drifted from our spiritual core and toward the drama, or illusion, we call "reality." The world of the moment places no importance on the physical or material, other than to accept that they are part of this human experience we call our lives. However, to fully embrace and enjoy all aspects of this experience, we must first find the place within, where our true self resides. We must return to the center of our very existence, and rediscover the inherent knowledge that is buried beneath the layers of conditioning we have been applying, coat after coat, throughout this lifetime. We rediscover that which does *not* change.

Our ancestors knew nothing of the technological, high-speed miracles that we witness every day, but they did know these truths thousands of years ago. They have not changed and they exist today in a variety of ancient traditions around the world. In order to reconnect with these truths, we can choose to embark on this journey within. As if peeling back the layers of an onion, we continually discover a new level of our selves, beneath the last. Each level is more pure, more free, more knowing, more loving, more peaceful and more full of joy. All this exists ... in the moment.

The poetry and prose that you are about to experience were written over a period of some twenty years. It represents a selection of writings that originated from my personal voyage of discovery, from my own realizations, observations, and from what I came to understand as simple, universal truths. I encountered and overcame my own demons, and developed an intimate relationship with my Self. I found peace and happiness, wisdom and clarity, and learned that these things *never* change. I embraced pure truth, faith and love, knowing that all these things exist only when we are fully present in the moment. Eventually, it became clear to me that abundance and prosperity was not related to "possessions" but to a consciousness, or a "flow," and that being in this flow, was a direct byproduct of *being* in the moment.

Each part of this book connects with truths representing one of those levels of the Self and relates to aspects of our spiritual selves that never change. Each section speaks with the voice from that perspective. *In the Moment of Life* ... honors all life as one, respecting and acknowledging that each of us is an integral part of the whole. *In the Moment of Self* ... honors the connection with, and the loving of, one's Self. Here we recognize and embrace that this same Self exists within each one of us. *In the Moment of Truth* ... is the heart of these writings and honors the direct connection each of us have with our God and provides insight into the true nature of Intuitive Wisdom that dwells within us all. The final part comprises four works that were created during moments of pure clarity. *We Are You, Slice It Away, In the Moment* and *Don't Stop ... Keep Going,* were all created when I was in direct communication with my highest Self, and they are the words of truth that came to me from within.

In order to enter the world of the moment, it is necessary to leave behind the conditioning of our past and attach to the part of us that never changes. We must remove the shoes of judgment, blame and criticism, and walk barefoot through fields of faith, love and truth. This is the wilderness of our dreams, where our intuition is our guide, and where we accept that every experience has been both a lesson and a gift. We take off the mask of ego and pride, and trust our inner Self to provide for us and protect us. Disrobe from the cloak of anger and fear, for this belongs only in the drama and has no place in the world of the moment.

As you walk through this door, release all issues of the past and all thoughts of the future. Detach from skepticism and negativity and attach instead, to the faith that dwells deep within your soul. For, in the moment, all things are possible, all dreams come true and all prayers are answered. In the moment, abundance and prosperity are our birthrights, and pure love is the most powerful force in the universe, which resides within each one of us.

Once you proceed on this journey, open your eyes, your mind and your heart. Be open to change, for your life may never be the same again. Be open to the opportunity for growth, and become aware of that inner part of you that demands your attention, but which you may have been neglecting. It is possible for you to discover your inner child, or meet your inner guide. You could even create a unique and intimate relationship with either … or both.

Welcome to this journey as we now join hands and become traveling companions from this moment on …

# PART I

IN THE MOMENT OF LIFE

## MOMENT BY MOMENT

Moment by moment ... we live

Hour by hour ... we work

Day by day ... we learn

Month by month ... we grow

Year by year ... we age

But ...

Moment by moment ... we live

## NOW

The time comes, once again,
To roll back the lid
From the box of memories
That has been left covered all these years.

What was in the present, is now in the past
What was in the future, is now manifest in the present
What will be of the future? ...

Will we become of our expectations
Will we become of our fears
Or will we simply become as much as we are

For in the future, all there will be is the now
In the end, all we will have left is the past
But now we can be as much as we are

Shake loose from the bondage of what was
Liberate the spectrum of what can be
And stay with the thoughts of what you believe

Your beliefs will carry you up
Up where you always belonged
Where thoughts are things
Where all things are possible
Where time is buried in the past
Where the past is buried in time

Now turn around ... look at the past once more
It's who you have become
Then return to now,
Accept the memories as the truth

And breathe in reality

Now you can go forward with the new
And be as much as you are

## THIS IS THE TIME

This is the time
when we say goodbye
goodbye to the past
where all is etched
in who we are today

This is the time
when we bid farewell
farewell to the crutches
we've been leaning on
far too long

This is the time
when we clean away the dust
the dust left clinging
to the anchors of the past
the barriers to the future

This is the time
when we must finally say
say that we love
who we really are
and acknowledge that today

This is the time
when we open the door
the door to our soul
sweep out the dark
let in the light
and enter our new beginning …
together … now!

## THE DRAMA

The drama unfurls
revealing its truth
as night turns to day
cementing its view

The drama exists
to keep us aware
of the life we would live
if we hadn't a care

The drama loves us
to keep it alive
to feed it our ego
so that it may thrive

The drama lives on
despite what we say
until we lay to rest
at the end of the day

## THE BOX

As the box opens up
All the ghosts are set free
You've been blind for too long
At last you can see

One by one they fly by
And greet you with a smile
Then they say goodbye
And they're gone for a while

Keep the box open
Let them join the light
Give them your love
Thank them for the sight

Let them fly free
For as long as they will
Climbing higher and higher
Gaining strength for you still

Thank them for all
The gifts that they give
Thank them for living
The life that they live

When the last one is gone
Close the lid tight
Then dwell with them always
Forever, in the light

## **STEP OUT OF THE MIST**

Step out of the mist
and into the light
look back at the fog
swirling around your plight

The storm is the illusion
the hurricane fear
the whirlpool of drama
seems evermore near

Take a good look back
to where you came from
then remember your task
… to find your way home

For it is only in the light
that you can possibly see
who you really are …
who you really want to be …

## THE SPIRIT OF THE NIGHT

The spirit of the night
Gives rise to our fears
The spirit of the night
Opens the door to our years

We are thankful for the day
We are grateful for the light
As our soul surrenders
To the spirit of the night

## **NOW IS ALWAYS HERE**

If we can slow down …
Stop … and think of days gone by
What are the thoughts that run through our minds
How often do we ask ourselves "why"?

Today is beautiful, but
Compared to yesterday, tomorrow, or what?
It seems the same in many ways
… but if we're truly aware … it is not!

All our yesterdays simply exist
As pieces of our life today
Our tomorrows will always bring hope and growth
The thing we never know is which way.

What does it matter … while we're here looking out
Sitting cross-legged in the den
We know it gets better … be patient … you'll see
The problem is knowing just when

So, think about this … when all is amiss
And confusion soon brings about fear
Just stop … look around … at where you are now
Because now … is always here!

## THE SPIRAL TURNS

The spiral turns
Ever increasing
In size ... and awareness

Its conscious energy
All encompassing ...
Passing
From generation to generation
As it evolves ...
Into the ultimate perfection
Of love and support

It gives unconditionally
And flows with peace and harmony
On its joyful progress
To eternity ...

## **FROM TIME TO TIME**

From time to time
It's nice to disappear
To run and hide
From the human race
To fall back ...
To peer from behind
The mask we call
Our human face

To become invisible ...
To blend right in
To the place you call home ...
Away from the race

But ... there's nothing like being alone ...
With another ...
Who's in the same place as you
Then it's hard
To try and describe being alone ...
... when there's two

You see, the bottom line is
When the truth you must face ...
It's nice to drop out
From time to time
... just to get back in the race!

## THE SOUL OF THE NIGHT

the light fills the soul
the stars fill the sky
the moon guides the path
beyond the reasons why

aroma fills the air
spirit fills the night
the sun is gone for now
as faith creates the sight

the moment lives for now
the memories live forever
we trust our souls in darkness
ready to deliver …

## ANOTHER YEAR GONE BY

Another year gone by
Fleeting and whispering
Its over-zealous speed to eternity
Taking with it thoughts of before
Memories left in the garbage pails
Stacked and stored
Waiting for spring cleaning
Reflections are transparent
And it's time … once again
To dust away the cobwebs
Left clinging to the tightrope
We walk each year.

## **IT …**

It cannot be returned or replaced
It cannot be bought or sold
… but is always spent
It has no beginning and no end
It comes when we least want it
It flies when we need it the most
It is killed … it is used
It is wasted … it is abused
It has always been too short
… and will always be too long
It is that of which we all want more
… but must always settle for less
Without it we could not survive
It is the most valuable possession
known to mankind

It … is time

## THE STORM BELOW

As the turbulent ravages
Echo in my groin
The spectacle performs and gloats
Over the myriad of lights below
It bounces the mereness of man
Like a ping-pong
Until its impact is felt
Down to the soles of our souls
It foreplays with our immortality
Teases our sixth senses
Rejoices in our inevitable vulnerability
Just can't resist its sadistic taunt
While generating its playful jaunt

That's what it takes
What recession …
What squeeze …
What health threats …
What political turmoil …
What apocalyptic environmental debacle
could possibly befall …

When all that matters
Is the storm below …

## **PLEASE DON'T TRY**

Please don't try
    to understand why
    in the course of our lives
    we must experience loss

You see, it's only through losing
    we can begin choosing
    the difference between
    living and death

On the road we call life
    don't expect freedom from strife
    for we cannot have the good
    without first knowing the bad

So, live while you may
    and think what I say
    in those painful times
    of desperation

And remember one thing
    the fear some now bring
    from ideas in their head …

    … maybe they're already dead!

## ONE STEP BACK

Just one step back
Through time and space
To where it all began
And reflections of what was
Are simply the passage of time

Just one step back
Gives you the chance to see
The place you are ... once were
The place you want to be

Just one step back
Every now and then
Will provide all the answers
To questions you didn't even know existed
Before it all began

Just one step back
That's all it takes
To find the truth
Behind the feelings
That clouded it all ...

With just one step back
You, too, will find
The treasures now hidden
In the shadows of your mind

## WANDERING

Wandering in the mire
      of the insanity
Enveloped in the feelings
      of the past
Surrounded by the music
      of the wind
Convinced that these days ...
      will not last

Can we give ourselves
      up to the heavens
Must we continue
      on a path in the mist
Have our tasks
      been completed here yet
With our dreams
      still left on a list

Just do it ... they say ...
      live in the now
Seek the truth
      and keep yourself whole
Forget the daily grind
      of meaningless activities
Keep on the path ...
      to the seat of your soul

Fine words ... we know ...
        when the strength goes away
Keeping the "faith"
        during the darkest season
To live with these thoughts
        is the push and the pull
Waiting for the light ...
        is the only reason

Give thanks for the lessons ...
        for the time ... for the faith
For sights ... for sounds ...
        for strength ... for light
For companions ... for health ...
        for family ... for love
And for dreams that come true
        by day ... and by night!

## IT'S TIME

It's time ... once again ...
To roll back the layers of darkness
Surrounding your light
Examine the depths of delusions
The sanity of the soul

The change is overwhelming
The start ... an awakening
The goal ... to survive a life
Made of lessons

Keep the treasures of the past
In the library of the mind
There lie all the answers ...
From eternity
To all the questions ...
Through eternity

One layer at a time
The skin sheds its death
Senses become grounded in cosmic light
Thoughts navigate the seas of uncertainty
As they seek the next plateau of sanity

Among the raging storms of doubt
Truth is the sanctuary
Love is the pathway we navigate continuously

We want to let go
And fall through the heavens
We want to hear our hearts
Alive with the prayers of the past

We want to usher ourselves
To the endless sunsets
Given to us as the guiding light

It's all stop ... and start
It has no beginning and no end
It gives less than we want
It gives more than we need

Needs and wants
Wants and needs
To want the needs ...
There lies the truth

What we need is all we must want
Give us the time to want only
What we need ...

*We need to float*
*In a cloud of calm warmth*
*We need to be bathed*
*In healing light*
*We need to fly*
*In our dreams*
*Until we can dwell there forever*
*We need to seek*
*Only truth and love*
*We need the gift*
*So we can give*
*We need this moment*
*To never end ...*

## THEY SAID …

They said …
It couldn't be done
    … it was

They said …
It wouldn't happen
    … it did

They said …
Never again
    … they were wrong

Who are they? …
With their all seeing blindness
    all hearing deafness
    all knowing stupidity

They speak without listening
    look without seeing
    hear but don't understand

They are cruel
    thoughtless
    reveling in the sorrows of others
    gaining joy from others' misfortunes

They see the negative with every opportunity
the sickness in every healthy situation

They slander
They libel
They spit when you're up
They kick when you're down

They are the product of ourselves
They are the black sheep
      the Satan
       the demon
      the devil

They are death ...

They ... are us!

## **NEW YEAR**

the vision that surrounds us
both dark and light
keeps the hope alive
that we can be wrong or right

even after the dawn
when day takes its break
and the wonder of life
is for you to take

follow the right path
though there are many to choose
only when you are done
can there be no win ... no lose

give it your all
especially at the dark turn
to raise yourself up
to where you belong

with the strength from within
you will follow your light
never wondering again
what is wrong ... or right

## **MONSTERS IN THE DARK**

Monsters in the dark

Become Angels in the sky

The moment the light is on

## LIKE IT ... OR NOT

Take a step back
    ... to yesterday ...

Drift in the backwaters
    ... of today ...

Peer behind the scenes
    ... at what was ...

And wallow in the memories
    of those glorious sunsets

Now enjoy this collage of thoughts
    ... this myriad of colors

Because the picture you'll paint
    will be your self portrait ...

Beautiful and perfect ...

Like it ... or not!

## FOOTPRINTS ON THE WATER

The ripple of the wind
    the waving of the light
    the glinting of the sound
    as the day turns into night

    The clouds from pink to grey
        the sky from blue to black
        the cool air lets us know
        the stars are coming back

        A perfect day of moments
            mother earth and her mother
            both touched by eternity
            and the footprints on the water

## MOONSTAR

What do you see, Moonstar
        up there in the sky?
A world that is troubled? ...
        yes ... but don't ask me why

You've seen us all come
        you'll see us all go
But, how ... and when ...
        is what we want to know?

What was it that started
        war, hatred and famine ...
And where should we seek
        the One to examine?

Look at me, Moonstar
        and don't try to hide
Those secrets you keep
        on the other ... your dark side

Was it you who changed
        the color of man's skin
And turned him around
        so he'd lose where he'd been?

And what of the tongue
        in which we all speak
Come on now, Moonstar ...
        it's all a bit "antique"

If it was you who made
        us mere people down here
Into woman and man
        from what did you fear?

It's time to own up ...
        tell us who you really are ...
Because nothing lasts forever ...
        not even you ... Moonstar!

## A DRAMA

A drama unfolds ...
    line by line
    scene by scene
    act by act

The writer is the director
The director, the writer
The actor performs
The audience observes

Each has their part in the "play"

The director controls the play
    writes the script
    auditions the players
    commands the action

The director decides
    when to be angry
    when to be happy
    when to confront
    when to let go

The director chooses
    who will be the victim
    who will be the hero
    who will be the villain
    who will laugh
    who will cry
    who will live
    who will die

The director changes
>	the script
>	the performers
>	the acting
>	the ending

The players are chosen
>	to act their selected roles
>	to play the parts
>	to perform
>	to be directed
>	to be controlled

The players are told
>	when to be the victim
>	when to be the hero
>	when to be the villain
>	when to laugh
>	when to cry
>	when to live
>	when to die

The players must
>	follow the script
>	be the performer
>	play the role
>	accept the ending

The audience member sees it all
>	watching and listening
>	can laugh or cry
>	can stay or leave
>	can be involved or detached

Which are you?

Are you directing your own drama?

Are you performing in someone else's?

Are you observing from a distance?

This is the time to decide your role
        and the roles of the others
           in the drama
you call your life …

## THE CITY

these are lost souls
they came here out of fear
they gathered together
and supported each other's pain

they believe in scarcity, not abundance
the energy of the city oppresses
shifts them away from God and spirit
everything in the city is man-made
not God-made

how else can they behave …

shifting from one foot to another
from one day to the next
as getting through the day is the goal
not the journey …

## **TURBULENCE**

It's smooth ...
like glass on a windless day
It's floating ...
in a cocoon of tranquility
It's motionless ...
at the speed of sound

The memories of the day nestle
into the sanctuary of their foreverness
We sail in space
chasing the elusive glow of tomorrow

Shudder ... shudder ...
The tropospheric restlessness
of the power whose space has been invaded
I SAID SHUDDER ... !
This time she meant it
She is woken from her meditative snooze
by this chunk of toxicity disturbing her very home

She's angry ...
As we attempt to indulge in social intercourse
She is offended by our poor manners
Our inability to wait until SHE was ready
BANG ... she spills ours drinks
WHAM ... the plates slide from our tables
We each glance briefly at another
Only to find a similar glance returned
Looking for the face of the seasoned traveler
saying "how tedious ... damn turbulence!"

Now she plays with our sheer hopelessness
She toys with our total vulnerability
Tosses us aside with contempt
as if we were just another feeble competitor
Unworthy of even sharing
the same space as her

She indignantly wrestles with us
like a cat tormenting a defenseless cricket
And with the same indifference
she pushes us aside
when we have outstayed
our welcome

She is bored with us
No more shudders
No more bang
No more wham
Back to the smooth, motionless float
Ping! ... "You may unfasten your seat belt
and move around the cabin ... "

I stare into the window at invisibility
At nothingness
Into the inevitable turbulence ...

## IF EVER ...

If ever there was a time to trust
It is now
If ever there was a time for thanks
It is now
If ever there was a time to love
It is now
If ever there was time to give
It is now

Now, when anger abounds
And doubt fills the air
When judgements run rampant
And the critics thrive
When pain is the symptom
The product of fear

If ever there was a time for surrender
It is now
If ever there was a time for complete faith
It is now

It is never too late
For now is always here

# PART II

## IN THE MOMENT OF SELF

## MOMENT OF THANKS

Thank you for this moment
this magical moment
when all of life is illuminated
when all of the universe is opened
when all prayers are answered

Thank you for the gift of my self
for the gift of all that are present in my life
for the gift of all events
for the opportunities to live in truth and love

Thank you for sharing universal abundance
for the creativity I enjoy
for the love that I feel
for the happiness that exists in my self
and all others

Thank you for this peace
for this calm
for this tranquility
for this moment

## **PICTURE PUZZLE**

My life is a picture puzzle
with colors and shapes
and darks and lights
with mountains and oceans
and scenic views
with rain and clouds
and sheep and cows
and trees and fields
and scapes of gold

My picture puzzle is real
if I look at the whole
... if I look at the whole
But, when I take away a piece
and look at the hole ...
what is more important? ...

Can it be the piece itself?
it's blue ... with shape
but where's it from?

The sky is blue ... so is the sea
and this piece on its own
could be either

If I look at the whole
what do I see? ...
... a space where the sky should be? ...
or maybe the sea ...
and if I look too closely
I really can't tell
because all I really see

is the hole ...
not ... the whole!

When I stand back
and view the whole
the space where the sky should be
need not be filled
for I know it's there
it's just missing
... for now anyway
And the picture is my life
And my life is the whole
... not the hole!

## I AM HERE

There's a simple truth
Encompassing life
I've arrived at this place
I am here

I am my parent, my child, my self
I am my mind, my body, my spirit
I am the earth, the sky, the universe
*I* am here

I am my being, my doing, my soul
I am my energy, my thoughts, my deeds,
I am action, love, creation
I *am* here

I am the present, the light, the path
I am faith, joy, peace
I am this place, this time, this moment
I am *here*

Three simple words
Each with their own meaning
And together they are magic
For *I am here*

## PASSAGE OF TIME

My window on the world
Is a fantasy of time
With oceans to cross
And mountains to climb

I see things I must do
Promises to keep
Making living my work
With only time left to sleep

One day I'll look out
Who's face will I see
There in the window
… staring at me

The sun … the moon?
Yours … or mine?
Or will I have witnessed
… the passage of time?

## **WALK ALONE**

I walk alone on a path all have traveled
I float in calm amid a stormy sea
My light shines bright when the fog does shroud
In the fear of my darkness I can now truly see

I climb higher and higher
Gaining strength ... all is clear
While this moment of perfection
Is ever more here

I've become of this place
This moment in time
I've become of this self
with my spirit in line

I can stay here forever
for this is my choice
I have discovered my truth
It's expressed with my voice

It means I must leave
my former self in the past
for I've arrived at a place
where tranquility lasts

## HEY WORLD

Hey, World

D'you think I don't know
what you have done to me
I opened my eyes and saw my reflection
the day the river reached the sea

D'you think I'm blind …
well, not any more
Because I found your key
and unlocked your door

Take care, my world
I don't have my head in the sand
I'm simply stating my case
… taking a stand

Hey, World … look out
you can't fool me no more
'Cause I found the key
… so open your door

D'you think I'm not ready
well, listen to this
I've aimed for your heart
I'm not going to miss!

So, open your door, World
let me walk right in …
Because, you're THE ONLY one
who knows where I've been!

## DEMONS OF THE MORNING

What do they do
When we first awake
These demons of the morning
When our memory they do take

They surprise us so
When our eyes first reveal
They want us to forget
Who we are ... what we feel

They criticize and blame
They judge and they eat
At our very soul until
We cower at their feet

These demons they love us
To stop and fail
They love it when we admit
We are chasing our tail

They dwell deep within
And awaken at night
Just so they can show us
Our doubts by daylight

They've grown, you see
Since I was a child
Feeding on my fears
As uncertainties grow wild

They only come alive
Because I allow them to
Because my demons are habits
That awake when I do

So now ... when I wake
And they invade my morning ...
I simply exhale my demons
... without any warning!

## **RAGING STORM**

There's a raging storm down below
Losses and pain
Continue to grow
Strength from within
Takes me by the hand
Leads me forward
To the "promised land"

There's a fire down below
Just trying to spread
Consuming my life
Destroying my head
Lifts me above
The reality of being
Opens my eyes
To the truth of seeing

There's a movement of the Earth
Shaking my core
Revealing the light
Opening the door
Questioning my spirit
Doubting my faith
… restoring my beliefs …
… knowing I'm safe

## SIGNS

If only I had read the signs
All the results would have been foreseen
If I had only read the signs
The impact would have been clean

Turning back the clock doesn't mean you're wrong
Going back in time doesn't mean change
If I had only read the signs
This feeling wouldn't be so strange

The memories are clear
The pattern is the same
If I had only read the signs
There'd be no one else to blame

Give me one more chance
Let me fix what went wrong
I will try to read the signs
At worst, I will be strong

One more, one more, one more
I guess it's not a crime
When we stumble, and we fall
While trying to read the signs

If I only read the signs
I promise I will go
I will only read the signs
If you let me … I will grow …

## THE CALM

The calm that resides deep within
sends its ripples of peace
throughout my being.
The storms of the week
have disappeared over the horizon.
The light bathes my stillness
as I float up
and dance with the angels
that reside in my soul.
This truth completes my circle of faith
encompassing my ring of fear,
as the flames of apprehension dwindle,
flicker and glow
as mere embers in the night.

## THANKS

talk to me when I ask for the light
open your arms to me when I ask for the way
rest my head when I'm in your sight
hold my hand when I walk through the rain
give my heart when I have it to give
show my soul when I'm full of your love
thanks for the gifts
thanks for the love
thanks for the moment
when I know who I am

## COLORS

In the mornings I am white and silver
As velvety clouds float in the dawn sky
and rustic waterfalls shower their silvery
beads over my naked soul
I am born in the setting of a silver moon
and the glow of light
casts its moonshadows at daybreak.
Before the sun wakes the day,
I am pure and clean and white.
I am the light of the cosmos
filled with calm, peace and tranquility,
reflecting the perfection of my new born life
in the still waters of my sanctuary.

With the sunrise, I am golden
The universal power is inhaled
with the first breath of the day.
The energy is awakened and illuminates my soul.
My spirit dances in the golden light
celebrating the arrival of yet another series
of unexpected perfect moments.

As the energy rises
I become orange,
burning with desire and passion
to see the perfection in all things.
Growing in size, the ball of fire touches all,
enlightens, and dwells throughout the day
in my wilderness of light,
massaging my soul as it seeks and sees
all things again new.

As the setting sun retreats from the impending stars
I am purple, majestic and serene
I glow in the aftermath of ecstacy
as the warmth fills my heart
and my sight fills my soul.
Peace, tranquility and bliss
again flood the perfection of the moment
as the dust clouds settle
into the slumber of the dark, blue night.
The stars glow, once more, at my fingertips
as I am indulged by the rainbow of perfection
that was this gift of a day
and the universe casts its protective shadows
stilling my mind
allowing me to see clearly ...

## ANGELS OF THE SKY

They slip through me
and enter my soul
filling my space and time
these angels of the sky
take nothing and give love
show themselves
and give without condition
these soaring angels of the sky
they share their space
their ultimate space
with an unknown
a laugh, a smile, a gaze
… into the eyes
and the answer comes
… suddenly …

## THE POWER WITHIN

There's a greater truth, a greater spirit
A greater power within
There's a force, I can feel
Just beneath the surface
It governs and leads from my innermost core
It demands to be heard
It demands to be seen and touched
And tasted and smelled
It demands to see and speak
And touch and hear and taste all that is life
All that is real

It is so much larger than me, yet dwells inside
It is so much louder than me, yet remains silent
It is so much more beautiful than me, yet remains unseen
It is so much more sensitive than me, yet remains untouched
It is so much more loving than me, yet remains unloved

It can see beyond eternity, yet is blinded by me
It sings a bird song, yet is silenced in my midst
It can paint heaven on earth, yet the brush is removed
It can open my heart, if I give it the key
It can open my soul and set me free …

All these gifts it can give
All this life it can live
All that is me it can see
All that I wish for it can provide
All I must do is stay out of the way
All I must do is let the power be
All I must do, is surrender, you see …

## WINDOW SEAT

From my window seat
I gaze out above the clouds
And marvel
At the wonder of creation
The vivid colors
Jagged formations
Curvature … heavens …

Closing my eyes
My thoughts drift to my inner world …
Frustration, anguish, pain
Fears, doubts, disappointments …

Colors fade to shades of grey
Sharpness of image blurring to haze
Things have not been going too well lately

And I'm wallowing in my self pity
My eyes open and drift across the aisle
At a man reading a newspaper
A business man … I think
Clean cut, forties, well dressed
Reading "The Journal"

A normal, everyday man
Happy … successful …

Then I noticed something …

He wasn't holding the paper with his hands
He was holding it with his … hooks!

This man had no arms ... prosthetics!!
My God ... what frustration

What anguish ... what pain
The man got up, out of his seat ...
No ... not the legs too?

Yes, the man is a walking quadriplegic

What fears, doubts, uncertainty ...

Suddenly, it all makes perfect sense ...
And my gaze drifts back to the window
At the wonders of creation
The colors and shapes
And I quietly thank the man
... and God

## MASTER OF THE MOMENT

Where do you go to
Master of the Moment
When I sense you're not there

Where do you visit
Master of the Moment
Tell me if you dare

Do you take a break
In that moment
Do you really not care
Oh, tell me
Master of the Moment
Do I have you to myself or
Is it with others that you share

When you're here
I feel your presence
You are like a golden light
Illuminating my way
Enlightening my day

You are a treasure, a gift
A mentor, a teacher
A parent, a child
Sent to show me the way

So, Master of the Moment
Tell me what to do
In order to fill my moments
Of every day with you

*Just close your eyes*
*Breathe deep and long*
*Let the flow begin and feel the calm*
*This is the moment in which you dwell*
*The moment that lives forever more*
*Stay in this moment and you will find me*
*resting in the shadows of your mind*
*and the wilderness of your soul*
*Ever present, ever yours*

Master of the Moment
I thank you once more
For tending my wounds
And mending my sore
For in this moment
I know you are near
And in the same moment
There is nothing to fear

This lesson of the moment
Is abundantly clear
My Master of the Moment
In the moment … is right here

# PART III

# IN THE MOMENT OF TRUTH

## ... TRUTHS ABOUT LIFE ...

there are no accidents
there are no mistakes
everything happens for a reason
there are no bad reasons
live in the present
do the right thing
do what needs to be done
want what you have
have no regrets
love yourself completely
be the most important person in your life

## MY GUIDES

Thank you for welcoming us into your soul
you have been with us always
and will be forever
this will *never* change

Be open to us always
and our strength will guide
now and evermore

Our light will shine on your path
and the truth will be ever more clear

## CLOSE YOUR EYES

Close your eyes
and dream once again
of the true magnificence
beauty and love of your being

The perfection of all that is
is around you and always will be

Whatever you dream is real
Whatever you call real is an illusion

Know this truth and grow

## THE LAST TIME

the last time I saw you
the world was small
even when we grew to this place
we were just a few feet tall

how can you ever pretend
to be who you are
when all the time
you are being just the same from afar …

come with me this time
join my colors … unite
be a part of my wilderness
forever … tonight

get a grip on now
for it's all we really have
take all there is this moment
for this moment's ever more

then climb to eternity
with the spirit of your past
and wallow in foreverness
with tranquility that lasts

## **DREAMS COME TRUE**

Look today at where you are
and try, if you may
to admit how far you've traveled
along the lonely path
to that perfect sunset ...

It's been so long, I know
since you've thought this way
but, you know, the time will come
Yes, you know, that in time you'll come
to truly appreciate even today ... one day

You'll be glad to reconcile ...
to account for the time you've had

So do not despair
when searching through clouds
Because it'll always be there
... just look a little further
when times get you down

And dreams *will* come true
if you really want them to

But ... *really* want them ... too!

## A CLEANSING

Observance, detachment, release, letting go.
Calm, peace, joy, happiness.
Clarity, wisdom, truth, love.
Light, gift, reflecting what is.

The past and the present
combine as oil and water
The flow of the past drifts
in with the tide as oil
washed again by the ebb
as water once again cleanses the shore

The recovery of the past,
the child, the truth
is in the cleansing of the shore itself.
This is not in action, but in release

You cannot make clean any more
than you can make a tree grow.
Cleansing becomes, as a tree becomes
The cleansing itself is the growth.

In every moment of growth
comes the dead of winter
With every moment of growth
comes the ebb tide
With every moment of growth
comes the rhythm of the universe,
the truth of what is flows in and out.
With every flow in
comes a greater attachment to truth,
a greater detachment to the past

Understand this flow,
it is where the peace is.
The rhythm of the energy flow is essential,
as is your acceptance of the energy flow.

In and out
Up and down
Back and forth

Be with the flow.
As wheat in the wind
As a rock in the river.
Let all this energy pass over you, around you.
It may even surround you.
It may encompass you.
In that moment detach.
See the truth and let go any sense of reaction.
Simply observe.
Be the rock, not the river
Be the wheat, not the wind.
Be anchored only in the permanent
not in that which changes

What is permanent?

All that does not change is permanent
Divine love is permanent
Truth is permanent
God is permanent

## THE CHALLENGE

As my life welcomes the challenges of the day
I am reminded that in the moment
there is no challenge
just action
just peace and calm exist
when we are in the moment

The challenge is nothing more
than an opportunity to demonstrate
what you have learned in your experience
An opportunity for growth
To be creative,
to love even more
to give even more
to release even more

The challenge represents the opportunity to see
and act in truth
to see what must be released
To let go to divine will
and trust that divine love is guiding you
along your path

Welcome the challenge
Be open, not afraid
See the gift, not the mountain
let your power work for you
let not your power be an effort
a force of will

Simply will your outcome
and release your power
No expectation, just safe in the knowledge
that everything is in rhythm
with the highest good of all

Melt the challenge, act in the highest good
Maintain the love that resides within you
and demonstrate this love in all your actions.

## OPEN YOUR EYES

Open your eyes, and let your thoughts flow freely.
They are the allies,
the friends that will take you to new heights
They keep you from hurting yourself
They protect and care, love and nurture
They create what you want, motivate what you need
Be aware of them ... open yourself to them

This is the time for all your energy to work together as one
Bringing forth all your ability and talent
Use your time wisely for it is limited, and be good to your self
Laugh and love, this is why you are here
If you do everything with love and keep it fun
What else is there?

Understand that deep within you lie all the answers
The river of answers flows through your soul
Be a part of the river, not apart from the river
This energy never sleeps, never dies
Just provides the source of all your beingness

Keep in touch with this "beingness"
And let your "being" become your "doing"
Do what you are as you remember who you are

This you will find, as you express,
and go beyond who you have been
Believe in your own energy to offer the gift that is you
As you open this up,
so will your awareness of others' gifts become clear

Trust in the intuitive touch of another
Let your soul guide you through the rapids
And rest you under the sun's light and warmth
Let your smile come from within and reflect your inner spirit
That which is love can never be hidden
That which is love can never be denied

Always remember that you are being guided and protected,
Loved and able to give love
To love your self is your greatest gift of all
At times of doubt, remember to love.
When anger, frustration, fear abound, remember to love
Love is the brilliant light which surrounds you
Which is you, which flows from you
Be love and see the love in all others.
Recognize and acknowledge the love in every thing.
They are all a part of you as you are a part of them
Not apart from them.
This will never change

All are part of the oneness that was created
All are vital and equal in the universe
Cannot separate one from another.
Must always know this and always honor this

Every day is your new beginning
Every moment is your new beginning
Now is your new beginning
Revel in your moment,
be a part of this, now,
and grow … to the end of your life

Your faith will always be your provider and protector

Come from faith, come from love

## THE GIFT

This wondrous gift
This night becomes day
This dark becomes light
This cold becomes warm
This earth becomes heaven

All things become as they really are
All lives exist as they really are
All souls remember who they really are

In this magical moment
Are all the gifts of the universe

See them ...
Feel them ...
Hear them ...
Be a part of them
Then ... never be apart from them
Become them ... as they become you

Feel the strength come from within
Feel the love of lives you've touched
And the love of souls who've touched you

This is the wondrous gift
This is the time for you to open
This is the time for you to receive
This is the time for you to let go
And let it be a part of you
Let it grow within you

Shed your light and love on it
Let it be with you always
As it was always intended

Let it encompass you
And all you survey
Let it breathe and give life
To all you know

Let it live as you forever

Remember ... this you know
This you believe
This you trust

Remember this truth
It cannot be denied
It's always there
You are the truth
... if you let it go
Become the truth once more
Grow in truth
Let wisdom be your guide

Let the magic flow forth
With abundance and love
Give with all your heart
Heal those in pain
Protect those who are lost
Light the path for those who do not see
Guide those who will follow
Your faith will be your guide

Trust your faith
Become your faith
Become who you are
Become your gift

## LET IT GO

Let it go
this grip you feel you must have
just let it go
you'll always be safe

feel strong within
and nothing can harm you

you're growing ...
to the end of your life
and it must be complete

keep all the memories
and store them forever
they're as much a part of you as your soul

keep all the thoughts
in your dreams
they are the future
any time soon

you have to maintain your belief
no matter what

give without condition
love without condition

that's all there is
*everything* stems from that

now ... follow your dreams ...

## YESTERDAY

Yesterdays have become today
Tomorrows are always there
In the depths of our souls
Lie the entwined mysteries
Of our lessons as they are

Things are always changing
Always learning
Always better

Cannot grow without pain
Cannot love without knowledge
Cannot know without growth
Must always be together

Accept the pain and grow
Revel in your growth
And know that *it* is all an illusion
Just a play
In the grand scheme of things
Nothing but love matters
Nothing but life is love

All things not connected with love
Are only temporary

Anchor yourself in love
And you will always be safe
Always out of danger in love

Be aware of the love you give yourself
Be aware of your love
Love your self
Love your soul

They are one ... and balanced
When you love your soul
Give yourself the gift of love
Love is light
Light is God
God is love
Love your God
And be in the light forever
You are protected in the light
You are protected by love
You are protected by God
At each time of day

When dreams become reality
And reality ... dreams
Surround yourself in light
And no harm will come

You are protected
Child of light

## **YOU CAN FEEL IT**

You can feel it now
  as this night becomes tomorrow
  as memories of your yesterdays
  drift through your heart

The closeness of your meaning

The meaning of your purpose

The purpose of your being

All incidents having now passed
  are recognized for the positive
  for the guidance
  for the lessons
  … be truly grateful

At last you are beginning
  to know who you are
  to like who you are
  to free who you are

You look forward to your tomorrows
  with open eyes
  with open heart
  with open mind
  and welcome it all
  with open arms
  ready to embrace
  the dawning of what you know to be

    the next great turn
    the next chapter in your book
    the next *plateau*

Transcending all thoughts of before
    their insignificance from the past
    is of great significance ... right now

Their meaning ... though confusing before
    now like *crystals* before your eyes

Their truth is real

Their reality ... truth

Your sense of worth and well being
    is growing ... even as you breathe

With each breath ... you get stronger
    with each move ... you live longer

Now you long to live tomorrow
    for tomorrow *is* the rest of your life
    tomorrow the sun will never set
    and you will allow the forces
    that have guided you this far
    to carry you up
    to raise you above
    to make you one with them

For now ... you are ready ...

## YOU KNOW HOW

You know how to walk
It's part of your being
As breathing in and out
It's nature's way

You know how to be
In every moment
As breathing in and out
You know the way

You know which is your path
With every step you take
As breathing in and out
You soul guides the way

You know the answer
When clouds abound
As breathing in and out
The light clears the way

You know how to love
When fear is the mask
As breathing in and out
Your heart lights the way

You know who I am
In each moment of doubt
As breathing in and out
I am the way

## LOVE YOUR SELF

Love your self
See the love shine
In all who touch your life

Smile into the light
And love that self
That exists in all others

This is the love you seek
This is the oneness that is
This is the way to completeness
This is the way to freedom

All these gifts are yours to be
and be a part of
Each moment of gifts
is in your awareness
Open your eyes and see it
as you open your heart to seek it

You are growing
That is all
The growth is magnificent
As it manifests in your being
Let the growth into your soul
And the light will fall on you
And shine through you
But first … you must
Love your self completely

# IN THE MOMENT

## IN THE MOMENT

Here it comes
as now becomes tomorrow
as all our gifts
join in this moment

Here comes the greatest gift of all
... the center of forever
This is the moment
we've all been waiting for
... the moment when
the light shines from you for ever more

You now understand
the real meaning of forever
for ever is now

Eternity is here
and exists for you in this very moment
feel the moment and breathe it
in the breath is this moment of forever

Be this moment
in the depths of your soul
for there it combines
with your life force

Have this moment
to share
bringing it as a part of you
to give whenever

Take this moment
as your own
and let it become you
as you become it
one ... together ... can never separate

Here is the love
Here is the light
Here is the source of it all

Everything else is an illusion
a figment of your own creation
a truth you have contrived
to fit the matrix
of the life you have designed
but not the life *we* have designed

You *must* understand this
for *only* here is the truth
of the moment

Become this truth
and allow the growth
to come through you

We want you to have *this* truth
for the answers to your questions
... here lie all the answers ...
... no shade in the moment ... only light
... no fear in the moment ... only faith
no uncertainty ... doubt ... disappointment
only joy and love exist
if you are *truly* aware

Open yourself to this gift
and *all* else will follow you
as you fulfill your life
with your own perfection

This moment is yours
to give whenever
and to have forever

Know this moment
and the light will always be with you

Love this moment
for that is all there really is

Be this moment
and let the light shine from you

See this moment
in others
for you to share together

Join with us in the moment
and you are complete
... cannot be anything else ...
for nothing else exists
in the reality

Do what needs to be done in the moment
and fulfill your dreams
for here is the *real* gift of you
the gift to you
the gift from you

This moment is our gift to you
Know this and you need never *know* of anything more

No push
no pull
no struggle
no pain

It's all here without condition

The greatest gift of all

Just accept and keep it with you
as your breath

The moment is the breath

The breath is the moment

Cannot separate
must always be one

Be one with it
and you can never be alone

You must know who you really are
move toward the promise you made
see the truth and stay out of the drama
know the answer as it exists in eternity
… in this moment …

Do not judge or blame
as you discover your truth

Let your life force guide you
on the path of consciousness
to help others help themselves

Let not your intellect deter you
from your goal or your truth

Let your soul know who you really are
and be true to your cause in this reality

Again and again
you *must* remember your cause
this will never change

... be aware
... be open
... be true

In this moment lies the real truth

No end to the truth

No end to the message

No end to the moment

Now ... take this gift
and grow to the end of your life
and love will follow you and this moment
... forever ...

SLICE IT AWAY

## SLICE IT AWAY

Slice it away
until you can see deep inside

Deep ... where it all began

Where the rot set in
and shut out the light

Slice it away

Until clarity is there
Until warmth fills the air
And the reflection of you
is passable ... acceptable

*Knowing* you is likeable ... amicable
Knowing you is loveable

*Love* who you are
when you *know* who you are ...

Who are *you* ? ...

Slice it away

Get below the surface

Feel the pain ... feel the hurt
It is good ... it is *so* good

It's good knowing you are able
Able to feel *you*
Able to know *you*

Though time and again
you cover it up
It's still there
... and always
You can't hide ...
You can't fight ...

Accept deepness of pain
The hurt alongside is good
Believe it is good and *grow*

Grow deep within and know

Know you ... and explore
the depths of you forever

Slice it away

Slice it away
and see ...

See what grows
under the rock
in the shadows
of those times gone by

In the history of your life ...
In the mystery of your life
lie the answers you seek

The answers you see ...
but still don't understand

Keep slicing ... deeper ... deeper

Colors are vivid

Greens and reds ...

Greens and reds
where have you been
buried so deep ...
so deep inside

Looking for light? ...

Grow now ... grow *now*

Now deeper and deeper

Moist ... warmth again
and again moist

Slice it away

So deep now ...

Now you can fall
Fall ... free
Free fall ...

No need to stop

Nothing to fear

Fall into colors

Into moist warmth
Into growth
Into expansion ...

Slice till you feel small
Small enough for your world
to be everything around you ...

The insignificant
becomes significant

The deeper you get ...

Get deeper and deeper

Know ...
Feel ...
Trust ...

Feel trust
Hold trust
Know you
Trust you
*Be you*

*Then* know you

Slice it away

Slice it away
until it's open

Open wide …

Feel good … feel deep
Feel deep is good
Then good is deep …

… we're there …

The center is around us

Around us is the center of forever

And now we see …
Now we understand
The beginning is all here
We have captured the beginning …

We have captured the beginning
but it has taken until now to find

Why? …

… because now …

… is the end …

… the end …

The end is now …

The end … is now … *the beginning!!*

Seeing the beginning
beneath the end

Deeper than the end ...

... again deeper

Deeper than the end

Slice it away

Slice away the beginning

Go deeper ... deeper ...

Deeper than the beginning

... the next beginning ...

Get deeper

Get smaller

Surround you with *you*
... and then you some more

Your world becomes you

So deep ...

... then ...

... then ...

... nothing ...

Then nothing? ...

Wait …

Just wait …

There's something …

I'm not sure what … but
… something …

… I'm … me

I'm me …

I'm universe …

I'm floating …
Communicating …
Transmitting … receiving … thinking …
Slicing deeper and deeper …

Now *I'm* the cutting edge

Now I'm slicing
Now I cut
Now I bleed
Now I choose …

Pain and hurt I no longer feel
Not a part of me

*I'm* the knife
Cutting deeper

Finding it ...
Finding what? ...

By request ... by order

Where's it been? ...

... ah ... here it is

I feel it now ...

Energy ...

Total energy ...

No push ... no pull

No care ... no thought

No need ... *no need!*


Have it now
Know it now
At last it's come
*I* have it now

Stay ... stay with me

Leave if you must
... but stay

I don't need you
... but stay

I know you
I love you
Go when you please
… but stay

I don't need you
… but stay

By request … by order

Stay …
… stay in my new beginning

Be a part of my center
Surround me
Orbit me

I am a speck
I am universe

Touch me with energy
With you

Think deep …
… deeper …
… now deepest

Deepest of all
is the true beginning

Here is the true beginning

Here … the start of it all

Weightless ... senseless
Knowing all feelings
Feeling no pain
Telethoughts ...
Telelife ...

Transmit energy

Life ... is ... all
All ... no ending
Just new beginnings

Yes ... at last ...

*The new beginning ...*

# WE ARE YOU

## WE ARE YOU

Close your eyes ... and clear the way
Clear the way for the love to come
With it will be the message
With it will be the direction

Open yourself to all this power
To carry you through and up
Up to where you belong
Through all this ...
... to the next plateau

Lift your spirit ... your soul
To the realm above
To all the other dreams

Creations are yours ... through me
And mine ... through you

We are one ... you and I

I cannot be without you
... nor you without me ...

You must believe and understand

That all this is part of us
No accidents ...
No dreams ...
It's all real
It's all really here ... and now
We're here ...

We're all here ...
... with you ...
Alongside you
You can't run or hide
We're always here for you ...

Whatever you need
You already have

Just to believe in us
Is all there is
This is where the rest is
The peace ...
The contentment ...
The love ...
The joy ...
The bliss ...

Be with us and see

All the incarnations of your life

Join with us once again
Until the true freedom abounds

But first ...
Be as much as you are
In the reality

Be with us ...
Let us be with you
We are one ...
All of us ...

Can never divide or separate
Waking and sleeping
It's all real
Cannot change a thing
Just go with it ...
... let it be ...

Open yourself to truth
And the pillar of support
Will be there
No way to stop it ...

You see ... we love you
You are love ...
You are complete ...

You must believe this
Then you can believe the rest
Trust in the rest
Become the rest
The rest is you
You are one with it
With us
With this ...
We are all one
Will always be one
This will never change

Be alone or not
You are never alone
Never can be alone
Too much going on
Too busy

Too loved
Too cared for
Too giving

All these gifts of the universe
Will come to you
And flow through you ...
Only if you allow them
Believe in them
Let them become you
Let us become you
We are you

Believe that and grow
Continue to grow
With us you must grow
We will never change

You are us
We are you

Be with us again
And fulfil your dreams
The answers are in your dreams
Live your dreams
Become your dreams
They are the true reality

Find us in your dreams

And there we will be one
United in eternity
Teacher and pupil
Each teaching ... and learning
Teaching and learning
Constantly lessons
No end to the lessons
... recognize them ...

Close your eyes ...

Feel the lesson ...

Go with your spirit
Your soul is your guide
The answers are in your dreams

Now ... dream ...
Dream ... and see the truth
And live the truth
... only the truth

That's all there is ...

**DON'T STOP ... KEEP GOING**

## DON'T STOP ... KEEP GOING

Give it up ... all of it

    even when you block the entry
    open it up ... all of it

Don't try or pretend
    even if you keep going, don't stop
    because it's there, somewhere
    trying to get out ...
    trying to release its innermost power

Strength to be free
    to be one ... to be complete

Don't hide ... don't run
    be ... just be

Don't stop ... keep going
    keep trying to be free

Be one with you ...
    be you with all

Take what you want
    when you have that to give

That is, what you want
    *is* what you give!

Don't stop ... keep going

You're nearly there ...

Just one more to go ...

In the next chapter you'll see
> the results of your efforts

Be one ... don't falter

Set up more than you want
> then what you need will be yours

Don't stop ... keep going

Just when it's dark
> turn the corner
> for tomorrow will be
> yet another fresh start
> in the never-ending changes
> you continue to sustain
> ... *if* you keep going ...

Don't stop ... keep going
> ... through it *all* ...

The pain, the tears, the fears don't stop
> just keep getting better ...

Better be there ...
> without them ... no life

Life ... is pain

Pain ... is love

Love ... is life

Must always be equal

Enjoy all aspects without guilt
    just accept ... and move on

Don't stop ... keep going

It's been so long
    since you had the chance
    to be this way

Don't ask why it stopped
    it may stop again
    but when it's good
    don't stop ... keep going

Go to the depths ... the outer limits

The shell ... is the interior

The outer limits ... never end


Don't stop ... keep going

Now ... is the external awareness

The vision ... beyond pain

The thought ... deeper than beyond

The completeness is there ...
        and always will be
        ... just clouded sometimes
        by uncertainty ... doubt ... fears

Comparing not necessary

*You are the best you you can be*

Take it to bed and be one with it!

Don't stop ... keep going

I'm asking you
        to take your courage
        and get a hold on time itself

Big time ... now time

Time to start the next phase ...

Return with me ...
        and your strength will grow
        ... will surround
        will help you help others help you

Keep going ... don't stop

You're getting closer ...
        closer than you've ever been
        ... it doesn't feel like it ... *it's O.K.*

Feel the surge come from within
        with smiles and strength
            and will it to be there always

Keep going now to all the ends
        to all the accomplishments

Smile ...
        and with you will always be
        love and friendship

Be confident ...
        be at ease with every situation

What you want ...
        will it ... and it will be yours
        no way to stop it

Don't stop ... keep going

We're going all the way this time

We find the answers
        to the questions of the quest

They're there ...
        just coming through the clouds ...
        ... one by one ...

In the light is the answer

No fears in the light

In the dark is doubt

The light is always there

Stay in the light

Don't stop ... keep going to the light

The *energy* is all powerful

The *steam* is strength

The *will* is your force-field and drive
Impenetrable yet vulnerable

Can feel pain

Can get hurt

And it's *O.K.*

Keep the smile
      and the light will shine on you
      then from you
      then *through* you!

Don't stop ... keep going

Even if there seems no more to say
      there's more to think
      more to be
      more to give ... more to take
      more to show ... more to see
      always more
      so, don't stop ... keep going

You will be shown the way through the darkness ...
    the tunnels will take you there
    there is no way around the mountains ...
    take the tunnels
    and through the darkness ...
    soon ... will come the light
    with the light will be the gift ...
    it will shine and glow ... even in the dark
    and you will smile
    because you will know it's yours ...
    yours to keep forever
    to give ... whenever

Know the strength and will that lies within
and nothing will be a barrier to your journey

There will be no mountains without tunnels ...
    no dark without light ...
    no light without love ...
    no love without pain ...
    no pain without tunnels ...

No need to stop
just the will to continue ... to keep going

There is *no* end to the journey
    that's why we don't stop

No end of thought ...

No end of you ...

*Only* new beginnings

The new beginning is *now* … and has begun today

Revel in your new beginning
        and smile into the light

And the next phase will reward your strength
        with the power from within
        power to be great … within
        power to accomplish goals … and live with them

Now … take my gift … and grow

Don't stop … keep going


Don't stop … *keep growing!*

*I held a moment in my hand*
*Brilliant as a star*
*Fragile as a flower*
*Carelessly, I dropped it*
*Oh God ... I knew not*
*That I held opportunity*


—Author Unknown

# PHOTOGRAPHS

Sunrise Moment · 1, cover

Restless Ocean · 7

Pathway in the Mist · 47

Millennium Sunset · 71

After the Storm · 95

Kelp · 103

Waterfall · 117

Golden Sunset · 125